The unmistakable outline of a class A4 — no 4498 returns from Coalville Open Day late in the evening of 5th June 1988, seen at Lockoford Lane, north of Chesterfield.

A. R. Kaye.

INTRODUCTION

The second volume of North Midland & Peak District Railways in The Steam Age covers much of the same ground as the first. The majority of the illustrations are from the former Midland lines, however, and many of the now vanished locations have never before appeared in print and those that have could hardly be said to have suffered over-exposure. Considering the size of the north midland area and the sheer variety of train types once seen here it is indeed surprising that so little has appeared in print. It is the intention of Lowlander to redress this situation, and offers of assistance in the way of photographs, anecdotes etc. will always be welcome for use in future volumes.

Thanks are offered to those whose work appears here, in particular the gentlemen mentioned on the back cover. They had the foresight to record the everyday happenings and decline of our once extensive railway system for which future generations should always be thankful.

A. R. Kaye
November 1988

SKETCH MAP OF THE AREA
COVERED BY THIS BOOK
(NOT TO SCALE)

The station buildings at Derby were rebuilt in 1987, and although the job has been tastefully done, it could never be a suitable replacement for the Midland Railway original, seen in the early 1960's when trolleybuses still passed the entrance. *Bob Tebb*.

The interior of Derby station in 1933 as Midland Compound No 1029 stands outside the original overall roof with an up express. *E. R. Morten*.

Rather drab platform awnings surround S.R. "Battle of Britain" 4-6-2 No. 34079 '141 Squadron' after its arrival on a special working in 1963. Noticeable by today's standards is the complete absence of railway enthusiasts who would normally be crawling all over such a distinguished visitor. *G. Newall.*

Heading south near Belper with an express for the Western Region is Bristol Barrow Road allocated Jubilee No. 45682 'Trafalgar'. This locomotive was a common sight on trains such as the 'Devonian' for many years, seen here in June 1952. *E. R. Morten.*

A long southbound mixed freight from the Matlock line creeps round the west to south curve at Ambergate with class 8F No. 48171 in charge. Note the oval platform indicator signs — a legacy from Midland Railway days. *J. R. Morten.*

A little known branch line in Derbyshire was that which used to leave the Derby-Sheffield route between South Wingfield and Stretton. It served the Colliery at Shirland and closed in the mid 1960's. This rare view was taken on a winter's day in January 1965 from the B6013 road near Higham. A standard class 2 2-6-0 runs light Derby to Shirland, the same scene today being part of a golf course. *Bob Tebb.*

The Wirksworth Branch was opened in 1867 and regular passenger trains ceased in 1947. The line continued to prosper until the early 1980's with up to three stone train departures each day. In 1988 the line is disused; it's future depends upon B.R. winning further contracts to convey stone. Failure inevitably means more heavy lorries on the roads. In happier times, the daily pick-up with No. 44920 waits at Wirksworth station before returning to Derby in May 1965.   *Bob Tebb.*

Stretton station used to be situated in the Amber Valley near the southern end of Clay Cross Tunnel. In this view dating from 1965, class B1 No. 61018 'Gnu' steams north light engine.   *Bob Tebb.*

A closer view of Stretton signal box and its Midland lower quadrant signal (left). Stretton station building (right) in 1965 after closure and awaiting demolition. No trace of the station remains today.

Bob Tebb.

Stretton signalman's view of a south-bound freight hauled by class 8F No. 48074 on 14th September 1965.   *Bob Tebb.*

Alfreton and South Normanton station used to be a much grander affair than the passenger would find today. It's modern counterpart is known as Alfreton and Mansfield Parkway but it is, of course, a good way from Mansfield. The old station was closed when local trains were withdrawn between Sheffield and Nottingham. Here it is at the end of the steam era with a class 8F running past from the Westhouses direction.

Bob Tebb.

Viewed from the bridge below North Wingfield church, an ex-Midland 0-4-4T hurries past on a Chesterfield-Pye Bridge local in 1932. The entrance to the Clay Cross Company works is on the left.

E. R. Morten.

Again from North Wingfield, but looking in the direction of Clay Cross Company, 4F No. 44122 propels a brakevan towards Clay Cross South, passing No. 44606 (numerically the highest) on an up freight in 1958. Note that 44122 is right-hand drive and 44606 is left-hand drive. *Bob Tebb.*

A general view of Clay Cross South junction and goods yard in 1964 as 8F No. 48678 comes north on a mixed freight. A 4F stands in the down sidings where one line used to continue into the Clay Cross Company premises. The sheds on the left still exist and house various old tramcars and buses, mostly the property of Crich museum. Clay Cross church spire may just be seen above the 4F's tender; the station was nearly two miles from the town. *Bob Tebb.*

After Hasland sheds closed, the Clay Cross shunting was carried out by Westhouses, and one of their 4F's No 44113 looks very smart as it waits at the south junction, on 4th January 1965.

The Clay Cross North distant is pulled off to switch No. 90013 on to the slow lines as it trundles a long freight off the Erewash Valley line. One of the Clay Cross Company's own diesels may just be seen in the distance. 20th August 1964.
Both Bob Tebb.

A rare photograph of Clay Cross Station looking south, dating from Midland Railway days about the turn of the Century. A Johnson 1F tank stands on the down relief line between shunting duties, and a 4-4-0 is on the down freight line. Note the porter perched on his ladder, engaged on lamp cleaning duties. *Author's collection.*

Clay Cross station buildings in 1966 just before closure, with one of Chesterfield's fleet of Commer parcels vans in attendance. The station closed on 2 January 1967 and was demolished in 1968. *Bob Tebb.*

Viewed from the down platform at Clay Cross, 8F No. 48421 has just crossed from freight to fast lines and makes for Derby with another lengthy train in 1963. *Bob Tebb*.

The view from Hepthorne Lane outside the station as Jubilee 4-6-0 No 45557 'New Brunswick' runs in with a Sheffield to Derby local train on 2nd July 1963. The town of Clay Cross was actually over two miles away. *Bob Tebb*.

North Wingfield church is again on the skyline as a Stanier class 5 on a summer Saturday extra is seen approaching Tupton. This view is not possible today, with the ever increasing vegetation at the lineside. *Bob Tebb.*

The Avenue Carbonisation Plant has always generated traffic for B.R. Extensive sidings were situated at Tupton from where the Plant's own locomotives would draw trains into the works. Nowadays, B.R. locos are permitted to take complete trains right in, obviating the need to stage trains in the sidings. In 1964 8F No 48200 stands ready to take away another load. *Bob Tebb.*

Opposite the Avenue Plant another branch line trailed off towards Grassmoor Colliery. This continued to Alma Junction where trains from Williamthorpe Colliery were staged. Beyond Alma, the line crossed the North Wingfield to Holmewood road at Highfields before crossing the fields to Holmewood Junction. Seen at Highfields Crossing on a wintry day is class 4F No 44355 as it struggles to restart a train of empties destined for Holmewood. *Bob Tebb.*

4F No 44603 was a regular on the branch until the last days of steam, pictured about to cross the road at Highfields. *Bob Tebb.*

On 26th March, 1964, No 44603 makes its way over Highfields Crossing, holding up a new Triumph Herald. This location is now the start of a new five mile footpath known as the 'Five Pits Trail' which uses the trackbed of this route and the former Great Central to Newton. Derbyshire County Council collected an award for returning the former routes to nature — a landscape 'previously disfigured by mine workings and old railways'. From Holmewood Junction, a line doubled back beneath the G.C.R main line and into the colliery but this section was operated by an N.C.B locomotive. W.D No 75175 drags loaded wagons up to the junction (upper right).   *Bob Tebb.*

The yard at Williamthorpe Colliery in 1967 with 'Jinty' No 47289 and J94 No 68012 being prepared for duty.   *Bob Tebb.*

A panoramic view of the colliery yard at Williamthorpe with 'Jinty' 0-6-0 No 47629 in the centre. A gang of workmen appear to have 'knocked off' whilst in the process of straightening out the right-hand track. The diesel replacement for the Westhouses steam locos stands further down the yard. Two steam locos were required at any one time, and Nos 47289/629 were supplemented by 47383 just before the end of steam, and most surprising of all, J94 68012 after closure of the Cromford and High Peak line. The latter ran under its own steam from Buxton to Westhouses, taking water at Chesterfield.
Bob Tebb.

Horns Bridge, just south of Chesterfield, was where the Midland, G.C, and L.D. & E.C routes could be seen. Austerity 2-8-0 No 90427 staggers southwards on a long mineral train.
C. Machin.

HASLAND LOCO SHEDS.

The entrance to the depot in Midland
days, with a 2-4-0 emerging.
G. S. Perrin collection/A. Bower.

The depot was situated to the south of Chesterfield near the Avenue Plant and supplied
the locomotive needs for local colliery traffic and for shunting at Chesterfield goods
yard. Main line work took the larger locos to Toton and Gowhole (New Mills). It was not
usually necessary to go into the confines of the roundhouse during the final years as the
roof and much of the retaining wall had to be demolished after storm damage and it was
possible to see everything from the surrounding bank. The shed foreman was not noted
for welcoming young spotters and the author remembers one occasion when he was
ordered off the premises in no uncertain terms. His name was duly taken when, some 30
minutes later, he was caught cowering in the cab of 0-4-0 No 47004. After several weeks
lying low fully anticipating the dreaded knock on the door by a member of the local con-
stabulary, he eventually plucked up courage to venture out to Hasland again only to find
to his dismay that there was not a single loco in sight — the depot had succumbed to
the inevitable; only memories would remain. This was the scene (above) meeting the
visitor to Hasland on a Sunday — a roundhouse full of filthy smoking locos. If only we
could still savour this today. Amongst those on view are 92081, 43982/6, 44355 and
47004.
G. Slinn.

A final look at Hasland across the turntable in about 1962. Regulars 44288/603, 47003/272 have Austerity 2-8-0 No 90714 for company. The depot closed in September 1964. *Author's collection.*

Tapton footbridge at Chesterfield has always been a popular spot from which to watch the local rail scene. This view across to the Spire in the early 1960's sees a northbound coke train double-headed by a 'Crab' 2-6-0 and 8F 2-8-0 — an unusual combination. The premises on the right were occupied at this time by a scrap merchant but were formerly the Chesterfield Wagon Works.   *C. Machin.*

In the other direction, the southbound 'Waverley' approaches Chesterfield with Britannia Pacific No 70033 'Charles Dickens' proudly wearing the headboard.

G. S. Perrin collection.

A truly evocative photograph of the down 'Devonian' as it storms away from the Chesterfield stop with Jubilee No 45699 'Galatea' in charge. This view dates from the early 1960's and shows the north bay platform where a D.M.U. stands ready to follow.

C. Machin.

The view from Tapton as class 5 No 44941 restarts a down express from the Western Region, and (below), Tapton Junction before more housing spoilt the landscape towards Lockoford Lane. Jubilee No 45575 'Madras' passes the local scrapyard where many locomotives were scrapped in the 1960's. How neat and tidy everywhere seemed in those days.

Both C. Machin.

A very rare visitor to the area in the shape of S.R 'West Country' No 34094, 'Mortehoe', seen passing Lockoford Lane on a special bound for Doncaster in 1964. *G. Newall.*

Another branch line ran from Dunston Barlow North on the 'Old Road' route, to Sheepbridge Works and collieries at Monkwood and Nesfield. A class 4F is seen coming off the branch and joining the line to Barrow Hill. The picture was taken from Newbridge Lane looking towards Tapton where a car-breaking firm now trades in the foreground.
G. Slinn.

These three photographs were taken in 1962 in the vicinity of Unstone and its signal box which was situated at the south end of the viaduct. A Royal Scot class 4-6-0 No 46148 'The Manchester Regiment' sets off across the viaduct, light engine, having most probably returned a rake of coaching stock to the nearby sidings after use on a Saturday extra. The lower view (opposite) shows that the photographer was able to secure a most interesting and extremely rare shot of class A3 4-6-2 No 60039 'Sandwich' on a Bristol-Newcastle express, doubtless a last minute substitute for a failed diesel. The picture was taken on a bitterly cold day from the signal box.

The signalman's view from the north as class 9F No 92166 runs briskly downgrade on empties from Gowhole to Avenue. Since this photograph was taken, trees have encroached upon the lineside and very little of the viaduct remains in view for today's photographers.

All G. Slinn.

North of Unstone, the main line briefly passes through open fields before reaching Dronfield. Seen from the bridle path to Summerley is a London-Bradford express as it storms the last few miles to Bradway Tunnel headed by Jubilee No 45616 'Malta G.C.'.

G. Whetton.

Once extensive sidings at Barrow Hill have now been reduced to practically nothing, and it is perhaps surprising that the locomotive depot still survives, although there have been closure rumours on many occasions. Barrow Hill depot is perhaps unique in that it is tucked away from the main line and it still boasts a roundhouse. This look at Midland Compound No 1117 dates from about 1933 in L.M.S days, and the depot may just be seen in the right background. Only the sidings in the foreground remain in 1988 — used for staging M.G.R trains from Markham Colliery, and a new automatic loader has been built to facilitate the removal of coal from the Dixons Opencast site. *Author's collection.*

Barrow Hill sheds in the early 1960's from the adjacent brickworks. On view are representatives of class W.D and 8F's with class 4MT 2-6-0's, the latter for working the Glapwell branch and local trip freights. *G. Slinn.*

Austerity 2-8-0 No 90544 shares the road at the front of the shed with a sister engine. The smokebox numberplate indicates that it was once allocated to the Western Region. These locomotives were known as 'bump-clanks' locally due to the distinctive sound produced by the motion. *G. Slinn.*

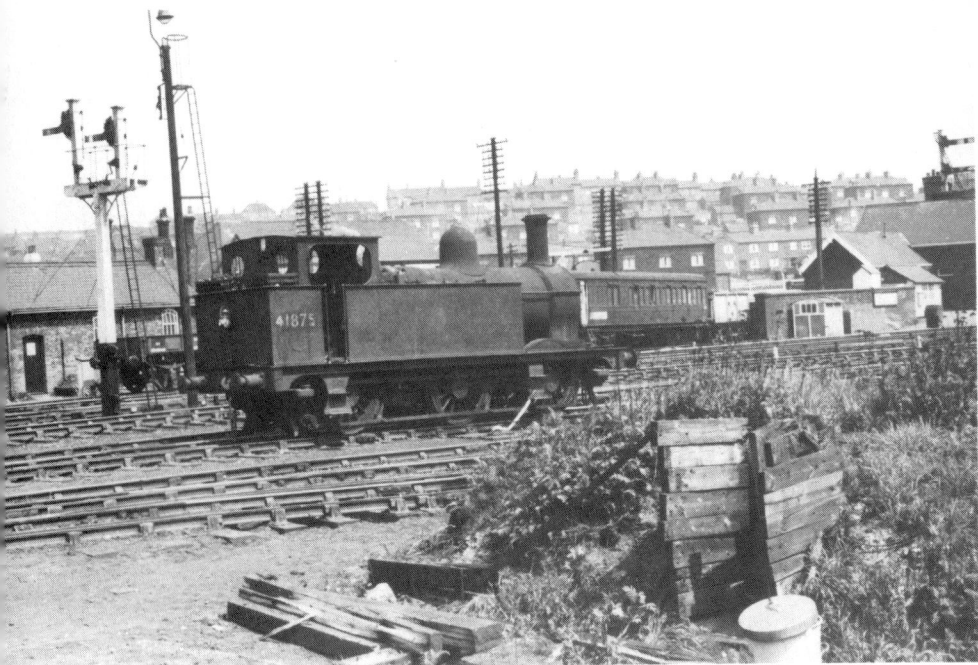

Barrow Hill became famous at the start of the 1960's as the final home for the Johnson 1F tanks operating at Staveley Works. A sub shed existed at the works and the B.R locos shared the accommodation with Staveley's own engines. No 41875, with enclosed cab, poses at the south end of Barrow Hill station before returning to the depot at the other side of the main line.　　　　　　　　　　　　　　　　　　　　　　　　*G. Newall.*

A rare look at Barrow Hill Station in 1933 as the down 'Thames-Forth Express' comes through with Midland 4-4-0 No 569 piloting a Compound. Notice how neat and tidy the station seems.　　　　　　　　　　　　　　　　　　　　　　　　*Author's collection.*

From Barrow Hill, the line to Seymour Junction veered off by Staveley Works. From Seymour, a single track continued to Cresswell, whilst another served Markham, Glapwell, and Ramcroft Collieries, as well as Derbyshire Coalite. Class 4MT No 43088 on Trip 62 working is seen at Seymour Junction in about 1964. At Bolsover station (below) class 4F No 44174 runs back from Glapwell towards the Coalite Plant. *Both C. Machin.*

SHEFFIELD
MIDLAND

Millhouses Jubilee No 45594 'Bhopal' makes a stirring sight as it starts out of Sheffield Midland at the head of a holiday extra for the Western Region in about 1960. *K. Smith Photographic.*

The original Sheffield Midland seen in May 1923 with a Lancashire & Yorkshire 4-4-2 standing at the head of a train from Bradford Exchange. Note the L.N.W.R saloon in original livery behind the tender.   *D.Ibbotson.*

Virtually the same viewpoint some 50 years later but this time Stanier 5 No 45404 is the subject as it waits with the stock of a local train for Manchester. Station pilot 61004 'Oryx' just manages to squeeze into the picture.   *G. Newall.*

The north end of Sheffield Midland before the monstrosity known as Sheaf House was built behind the station entrance. Class B1 4-6-0 No 61275 has charge of a relief train for York. *G. Slinn.*

Millhouses shed provided the station pilots for Midland, with a small stud of Ivatt class 2 tanks allocated. No 41245 was on duty at the north end of the station on 31st August 1961. *S. J. Kiziwicz.*

The view from the G.C.R bridge just outside Sheffield Victoria. Jubilee 4-6-0 No 45616 'Malta G.C' has just passed through Attercliffe Road station as it approaches the Midland on a Bradford-St. Pancras express. *G. C. Perrin collection.*

The final regular steam working out of Sheffield in 1966 was the 09.39 'all stations' to Chinley which employed one of Buxton's class 2 2-6-0's. No 46485 stands ready to depart from the up bay platform. *G. Slinn.*

In the days when prestige trains on the Midland bore headboards, Leeds Holbeck Jubilee No 45675 'Hardy' is seen on the climb out of Sheffield near Millhouses with the Glasgow to St. Pancras 'Waverley'. *K. Smith Photographic.*

Rather an uncommon choice of motive power for a down Hope Valley local is this 2-6-4 tank No 42379, seen climbing the bank at Millhouses with a full train. Millhouses sheds were situated to the right of the signal. *G. Newall.*

A rather misty day at Dore & Totley as class 5 No 44815 draws to a stand with a Derby-Sheffield local. The Hope Valley lines diverged here. Nowadays the layout here is much simplified, with the main line platforms gone and only the down side Hope Valley platform left. 8th April 1965.   *Bob Tebb.*

Back to the L.M.S era again, with this fine view of a down express hauled by a Midland Compound as it sweeps round the Dore south to Dore station curve in March 1933.
E. R. Morten.

This is the view looking north from Twentywell Lane bridge towards Dore & Totley station in 1963 as Jubilee No 45611 'Hong Kong' puts up a fine exhaust on the climb from Sheffield to Bradway Tunnel.   *G. Newall.*

A short freight for Earles Sidings takes the Hope Valley line and is about to pass beneath Twentywell Lane bridge. 8F No 48679 sports a Fowler tender.   *G. Newall.*

Until the closure of Hasland shed, class 4F's were regularly seen on Dore South to Dore West curves as they worked to Gowhole on trains from Avenue. Here No 43967 approaches the west junction. *G. Newall.*

Trains from Barrow Hill to Gowhole yard were not routed along the Beighton to Sheffield line (ex-G.C.R) to gain the Hope Valley route, presumably because they might foul the main lines in the vicinity of Sheffield Midland, and the Nunnery Curve has not always been a main line connection. Instead whole trains were unusually propelled down to Tapton Junction at Chesterfield from where they could gain the main line through Bradway Tunnel. Austerity No 90719 comes round the south to west curve at Dore in 1963. *G. Newall.*

Earles Sidings at Hope provides the Hope Valley line (or the Dore & Chinley as it was called after opening in 1894) with much of its traffic running to and from the cement works. It was this fact which led to the route being retained, whilst the line through Bakewell was to be closed — they could not, it was stated, both be operated as through routes to Manchester. In order to turn steam locos arriving at Hope, a turntable was provided just east of the station. The fireman of 4F No 3885 is obviously using every ounce of his strength to spin the loco round in July 1948.   *Author's collection.*

The well known location of New Mills South Junction is pictured in 1934 as a local train from Manchester via Disley Tunnel begins the climb to Chinley behind ex M.R No 485.
                                                                                      E. R. Morten.

This photograph will be of interest to those who are familiar with the activities of Peak Rail at Buxton, as it shows the present preservation site as it was in August 1964, seen from a passing train. *Bob Tebb.*

A railtour from Sheffield Victoria to Parsley Hay for the Cromford & High Peak line ran via the Woodhead route before continuing up the ex-L.N.W.R from Buxton. Headed by class B1 No 61158, the train is seen on the climb past Higher Buxton. *E. R. Morten.*

A view out of the same train as it approaches Harpur Hill — the photographer can be seen on the previous shot of course. The date of this trip was 29th August 1964.

Bob Tebb.

Photographs of the Cromford & High Peak have been omitted from this book as it is intended to publish one exclusively on this line in the near future. Returning to Buxton, therefore, and a view of another railtour, this time dating from June 1953 as 0-6-0 No 43387 arrives at the L.N.W.R side of the station. Note the superb signal gantry on the viaduct as seen from the signal box.

E. R. Morten.

Back on the Midland side of Buxton, but this time with a superb look at the end of the station (now the Peak Rail site), as ex-Midland 0-4-4T No 1247 arrives from Millers Dale, complete with dining car next to the loco. A March 1933 photograph. *E. R. Morten.*

A further look at the Millers Dale shuttle from Buxton, where passengers changed for London trains. Topley Pike bridge is featured in this view from May 1932 as 0-4-4T No 1350 passes over. *E. R. Morten.*

The older order at Great Rocks Junction in July 1933 looking towards Peak Forest and some of the quarry workings. Compound No 1064 comes down the bank from the summit on a Sunday train from Manchester Central. *E. R. Morten.*

In later years, a turntable was constructed at Great Rocks in the space to the right of the previous picture. Class 8F No 48365 stands here in the winter of 1966. The turntable base may still be seen in 1988, but it is usually filled with water. *Bob Tebb.*

Seen from the signal box at Great Rocks, a down express from London to Manchester romps up the bank in the capable charge of Britannia Pacific No 70021 'Morning Star' on a warm day in August 1959. The train has about one mile further to climb before reaching Peak Forest Summit at 985 feet above sea level. *E. R. Morten.*

Further down the bank, Chee Dale is reached, and up trains passed through Chee Tor Nos 1 and 2 tunnels before emerging into Millers Dale. Class 4F No 44429 heads a westbound freight across Millers Dale Junction on 6th September 1958. *E. R. Morten.*

Millers Dale station on 2nd August 1960 looking south as an up express stands in the platform whilst Fowler 2-6-4T No 42306 is parked by the Buxton bay platform.

H. B. Priestley.

The railway was carried high across the River Wye on a couple of impressive viaducts at Millers Dale. Class 2P No 40326 pilots a Jubilee 4-6-0 on the approach to Millers Dale Junction and the viaducts, in July 1954. *G. Whetton.*

A brace of 4F's, with No 4018 in the lead runs down the dale between Millers Dale and Litton Mills with a mixed freight on a beautiful September day in 1938. The scenic delights of the Peak line and the exciting photographic possibilities which would be opened up again if Peak Rail achieve their objective, may be appreciated with views such as this.   *E. R. Morten.*

Walkers are not permitted to pass through Headstones Tunnel between Great Longstone and Monsal Dale, but they may rejoin the Monsal Trail at the well known viaduct. Back in July 1958, class 8F No 48079 brings a westbound freight through Monsal Dale, banked in the rear by a 4F which seems to be doing all the work.   *E. R. Morten.*

A delightful study of Great Longstone (For Ashford) as 'Crab' 2-6-0 No 42874 comes through on a fitted freight. Note the L.M.S station sign. The stationmaster's house and down platform still survive in 1988, and the route between Bakewell and Millers Dale is of course known to walkers as the Monsal Trail. *J. R. Morten.*

This is the view from the road at isolated Hassop station looking in the Bakewell direction on 9th June 1968. The train approaching is the final steam working to use the line, hauled by Britannia Pacific No 70013 'Oliver Cromwell'. *G. A. Lilleker.*

At certain times of the day there were so many banking locos waiting for a path to return from Peak Forest to Rowsley that it became necessary to run them coupled together, and it was not unusual to find up to four travelling in this way. There was however, only a pair on this occasion as a 'Crab' 2-6-0 leads 4F No 44013 into Bakewell on 7th August 1958.   *E. R. Morten.*

From Rowsley, westbound trains began the climb through the Peak, and almost all freights took a banking locomotive. The gradient is apparent from this view of 4F No 4019 as it toils up Haddon Bank past Rowsley North Junction distant signals in July 1938.   *E. R. Morten.*

A class 5 4-6-0 comes through Rowsley North Junction with an up train in September 1939, passing a Johnson 0-6-0 which is occupied shunting milk tanks. Just beyond this point was the original yard and station, built in 1849, and the stone building may still be seen in 1988. It was replaced by a second station with the opening towards Bakewell in 1862. *E. R. Morten.*

South of Rowsley marshalling yards and loco sheds, the line passed Church Lane Crossing where a loop existed in which freights and local trains could take refuge whilst London expresses passed. Midland 4-4-0 No 537 leaves the loop and enters Darley Dale with an up local in July 1938. The station closed in March 1967, but the sidings have now been taken over by Peak Rail, and a short section of track may be seen for the first time in 20 years. *E. R. Morten.*

The Winster road at Darley Dale will need to have a new level crossing before trains can reach Matlock again. The old order as seen from the footbridge in about 1960 as ex W.D 2-8-0 No 90669 heads towards Rowsley where it will take a banking loco for the onward climb into the Peak. *J. R. Morten.*

Matlock looking north on 3rd April 1963 as 8F No 48191 approaches, passing the goods yard. Note the elevated signal box above the loco. This is the present extent of B.R operations, and a loop was retained for occasional excursion trains. Cawdor Quarry, on the left of the picture, has provided much traffic for the railway through the years, but although still thriving, it now sends out all stone by road. *Bob Tebb.*

Seen from the down platform at Matlock Bath, Jubilee 4-6-0 No 45649 'Hawkins' thunders past on a Manchester to St. Pancras express in May 1952. The now famous Heights of Abraham cable cars begin their ascent behind the building on the right in the 1980's. *E. R. Morten.*

An unusual viewpoint at Matlock Bath showing the goods dock and the High Tor grounds beyond. Class 4MT No 42228 waits in the station on a local for Derby. Originally closed in March 1967, Matlock Bath reopened in May 1972 and is served by the Sprinter railcar service to Derby. This photograph dates from November 1961. *Bob Tebb.*

Cromford in L.M.S days with an up train headed by ex-Midland Compound 4-4-0 No 1036. Fortunately the station buildings here have a preservation order on them, so they survive as a perfect reminder of Midland days. *Author's collection.*

Another Compound is piloted by a 2P as they cross the Derwent before entering Lea Wood tunnel with an up express in June 1938. *E. R. Morten*

NOTTINGHAM-WORKSOP.

With the announcement in 1988, that the old Nottingham to Mansfield and Worksop line may be reinstated, a reminder of the final days of passenger trains in the 1960's is appropriate. The last trains ran in October 1964, and this view comes from the final day of services. 4MT tank No 42218 is heading the train as it is about to enter Kirkby tunnel under the Robin Hood Hills. The tunnel was filled in during 1974, but recent excavations have revealed it to be in remarkably good condition.   *Bob Tebb.*

Another last day shot of Sutton Junction station looking in the direction of Mansfield as another 4MT tank draws to a stand with a train from Worksop. 10th October 1964.
Bob Tebb.

A Fowler 'Crab' 2-6-0, No 42822 (with Caprotti valve gear) moves out of the station and over the crossing at Sutton Junction North at the head of an excursion for Skegness in 1959. *Bob Tebb.*

Mansfield Town station buildings just prior to closure. It is said that the town is now the largest in the country without a train service, but should it be reinstated, the new station would probably have to be resited. *Bob Tebb.*

Under the overall roof at Mansfield, No 42218 blows off impatiently before moving off across the impressive viaduct on 10th October 1964.

The scene at the east end of Mansfield station as a Worksop to Nottingham train approaches with another 2-6-4 tank running bunker first.

Both Bob Tebb.

Back aboard the train again, as it sets off across Mansfield viaduct above the Market Place. *Bob Tebb.*

Shirebrook West seen from the train. The remains of this station may be found today, immediately opposite the diesel depot. *Bob Tebb.*

Differing station designs are seen as the train makes its way towards Worksop. This is the building at Langwith. *Bob Tebb.*

Whitwell station was demolished stone by stone in the early 1980's after lying empty for nearly 20 years since closure. It was transported to the Midland Railway Centre at Butterley, where it was rebuilt to serve as the headquarters and shop. *Bob Tebb.*

The sight of a class B1 4-6-0 passing Whitwell on a passenger train in the early 1960's was rare, and Retford allocated No 61212 was probably working a summer Saturday holiday train to Nottingham.

R. J. Buckley.

In the 1950's, the Nottingham-Worksop trains were worked by L.M.S (ex L.T.S.R. design) 4-4-2 tanks, represented here by No 41947 seen on the Tranker Wood curve near Woodend Junction, Shireoaks. *G. Whetton.*

After arrival at Worksop, No 42218 prepares to run round the train by running across the road at Worksop East. The picture was taken from the now demolished footbridge. *Bob Tebb.*

NORTHWARDS VIA THE GREAT CENTRAL.

The Great Central route from Nottingham towards Manchester has been covered in our companion volume, but its popularity seems to be increasing despite closure as a through route more than 20 years ago. For the purposes of this book, Kirkby South Junction will be the starting point. Situated just north of Annesley, the junction was actually a double one as seen in this view looking north. A class 8F comes off the ex-Great Northern Leen Valley line whilst the Mansfield route can be seen beyond the signal box.

Bob Tebb.

In Mansfield, the line from Kirkby to Clipstone cannot be traced at all in the vicinity of the Central station. It was virtually perched on an embankment and this has been cleared away. During August 1959, it was very much still in business as 'Crab' 2-6-0 No 42847 stopped to pick up day trippers most probably bound for Skegness. *H. B. Priestley.*

A most unusual visitor to the G.C. main line near Holmewood in 1963 as class 4F No 43918 heads north on a train of bolsters. These locos were of course the normal form of motive power just over the fence on the Midland branch from Avenue. *Bob Tebb.*

The G.C line has been completely wiped off the face of the earth north of Kirkby, and at Holmewood nothing remains of the colliery. The cutting where Holmewood Colliery box once stood is now a field. In August 1959, class K3 2-6-0 No 61882 also has a string of bolsters in tow as it passes the signal box. *Bob Tebb.*

Heath station looking towards Holmewood in October 1965 when the G.C line had but eleven months left before closure. Again, all trace of the railway has gone, and a new road and roundabout are to be found here — a new industrial estate now occupies the site of Holmewood Colliery, and a link road to the M1 motorway uses sections of the old Chesterfield Loop line.   *H. B. Priestley.*

The view from the G.C. footbridge towards Chesterfield at Horns Bridge. Class 9F's were practically unheard of on the loop, but one of the former Crosti-boilered examples was something of a scoop. No 92028 leaves Chesterfield Tunnel on 10th April 1962.
                                                                                    S. J. Kiziwicz.

The axe fell on the Chesterfield Loop on 6th March 1963, and this was the scene on that cold and miserable afternoon as the final passenger train to reverse into the north bay had just arrived from Leicester. B1 No 61094 would wait for about one hour before going forward to Sheffield Victoria at 16.20. The author has fond memories of the last months at Chesterfield Central, and hardly a single weekday passed without the usual trek down to the station after school to see what was standing at the head of the 16.20. More often than not we would be invited into the cab of either a B1, V2, or Stanier class 5 before it left — providing, of course, that we took our turn with the firing shovel. The aroma of freshly made sweets drifting across from an adjacent factory mingled with hot oil and steam. One can still stand by the new Inner Relief road and smell the sweets as traffic races by, but of steam locomotives and Chesterfield Central, only memories remain. A final look back (below) at Chesterfield Tunnel entrance and the station buildings on Infirmary Road. The frozen water tower bears testimony to the funereal weather on that most depressing of days.

Both G. Slinn.

A northbound departure to Sheffield Victoria hauled by class V2 2-6-2 No 60925 on 30th March 1962, seen as it approaches Wharf Lane footbridge with part of the goods warehouse just visible. *S. J. Kiziewicz.*

At the same time of writing, the area just south of Staveley Works station is an opencast coal mine known as Dixons, and, after eventual landscaping, a new Brimington bypass road may be constructed through here. In the meantime, here is a memory of ex G.C.R 4-4-0 No 5437 "Prince George" as it passes the signal box on a train from Manchester to Leicester in about 1937. *Author's collection.*

The exterior of Staveley Central which was situated on the bridge over the line at Lowgates. *J. H. Turner.*

This is the Chesterfield Loop platform at Staveley Central showing B1 No 61027 'Madoqua' having arrived on a down stopping train. Traces of the platforms may still be seen, but the remaining stub of main line, latterly running to Arkwright Colliery and disused since 1982, was finally lifted in the summer of 1988. Heavy subsidence meant that tracklifting trains could not be used, and demolition was carried out by means of one rail wagon — towed up and down by a mechanical digger. *Author's collection.*

STAVELEY SHEDS.

The following series of photographs show Staveley G.C depot as it was in the early 1960's prior to closure. There were rows and rows of grimy steam locos, some in steam, most in store. Four class 01's stand silently in front of the shed on a Sunday with Nos 63590/650 nearest the camera. The ex L.M.S types present were all former Sheffield Millhouses locos, made redundant by closure of that depot. Noteworthy was the fact that all still bore name and numberplates. Nearest the camera are Jubilees 45570/6 with chimneys sacked over. With the ever increasing number of locos out of service by the Autumn of 1962, space at depots such as Darnall was becoming hard to find and Staveley became the local dump.   *Both G. Slinn.*

Former Millhouses 'Royal Scot' class 4-6-0 No 46164 'The Artists' Rifleman' poses in the shed yard after being in store initially at Barrow Hill, whilst (below) rows of stored B1's totalling one dozen provide a sad sight, although many would see just one more summer operating season.
Both G. Slinn.

B1 No 61047 has Royal Scot No 46151 'The Royal Horse Guardsman' for company at the back of the depot yard, again in 1962. *G. Slinn.*

Meanwhile at the front of the depot but in service this time, was W.D Austerity No 90255 shedded at Doncaster. *G. Slinn.*

A nice clean B1, No 61316, is seen on the climb from Beighton towards Killamarsh Junction with southbound coke hoppers. *G. S. Perrin collection.*

The 14.17 Sheffield (Vic) to Nottingham headed by class K2 2-6-0 No 61728 is seen departing from Woodhouse 27th June 1959. This engine was allocated to Colwick — the turn being rostered to that depot. *J. H. Turner.*

The approach to Woodhouse East Junction in August 1959 as class 04 No 63783 trundles off the Worksop line with a down freight containing scrap metal.
J. H. Turner.

A little further south from Woodhouse was the extensive junction at Killamarsh. This is a rare view from the signal box looking towards the little known connection with the L.D. & E.C.R as an unidentified Britannia Pacific approaches heading the diverted down Boat Train from Harwich.
A. Rowles collection.

The 09.28 up express for Marylebone makes its way out of Sheffield past Woodburn Junction (below) with grimy A3 60107 "Royal Lancer" in charge. 8th August 1953.
B. N. Collins.

Sheffield Victoria some seven years after the electric wires went up. The Harwich Boat Train at this time was a regular March B17 job, represented here by No 61643 "Champion Lodge" as it departs with the up train on 6th April 1959. *J. H. Turner.*

The north end of Victoria as ex-G.N.R. class J6 0-6-0 No 64264 runs in across the Wicker Arches with a local train from Penistone on 21st August 1954. This was during the period when electric trains were being progressively introduced, and indeed anything Darnall had available could appear on these workings. *B. N. Collins.*

The Harwich to Liverpool Boat Train again, with B17 No 61626 'Brancepeth Castle'. This fine view was taken in February 1953 at Tranker Wood, Shireoaks, as the train accelerated away from the Worksop stop.

G. Whetton.

EAST COAST MAIN LINE.

Whilst featuring the eastern corner of the area covered by this volume, a brief visit to the East Coast route in the Tuxford region is appropriate. This is class A4 4-6-2 No 60030 'Golden Fleece' on a down express near Dukeries Junction. The L.D. & E.C.R line passes over the main line in the background. A March 1959 photograph.

Tuxford Station may just be seen towards the rear of the up 'Elizabethan' hauled by A4 No 60022 'Mallard'. Tuxford Junction leading to Dukeries Junction and the L.D. & E.C.R is behind the photographer. *Both: Bob Tebb.*

LANCASHIRE, DERBYSHIRE & EAST COAST RAILWAY.

Known as the Dukeries Route, this line was once connected to the G.N.R. at Tuxford, and there were extensive sidings and a wagon works in the triangle seen behind Britannia No 70002 'Geoffrey Chaucer'. This ex-works loco had just made a trial run after shopping at Doncaster and was about to set off back. 25th July 1962.   *Bob Tebb.*

Several Britannias were allocated to March in the early '60's for working fish trains from Grimsby. They would sometimes stray on to humble loose coupled freights, however, and worked onto the L.D. & E.C.R. from Lincoln. This is a rare view of 70001 'Lord Hurcomb' as it leaves Mansfield Concentration Sidings at Clipstone in July 1962. *Bob Tebb.*

Edwinstowe Station in 1954 sees W.D. 2-8-0 No 90732 on an eastbound coal train from the Mansfield direction. This loco was numerically the highest, and carried a commemorative nameplate 'Vulcan' on the cabside above its number. Local passenger trains between Lincoln and Chesterfield (Market Place) were in the hands of class A5 4-6-2 tanks in the early 1950's. This is Ollerton (below) also in 1954 as No 69815 prepares to leave for Shirebrook North only — the line westwards having closed to passengers in 1951.   *Both: G. Whetton.*

The Dukeries Route and the ex-G.N.R. Kirkby to Beighton (Leen Valley) met at Shirebrook North close to Langwith loco sheds. Seen from a farm bridge, B1 No 61004 'Oryx' brings an excursion bound for the East Coast across the girder bridge spanning the Midland route to Worksop. A row of class 04's may be seen in the yard opposite.

R. J. Buckley.

No mention of Langwith would be complete without at least one visit to the sheds. Here is part of the standard scene one could find in the early '60's with the place full of Robinson 2-8-0's. Class 01 No 63768 stands with an 04 near the coaling stage. The area today is part of the W. H. Davis wagon repair works.

Bob Tebb.

Scarcliffe station in the early years of the Century with the Station Master posing for the photograph with his children. The view is towards Bolsover. *Author's collection*

The last days of the Shirebrook-Chesterfield section saw trains mostly in the hands of class A5 tanks such as No 69812 seen running round its train at Market Place. The picture is from the signal box looking out over Markham Road and the Abattoir. This station closed on 1st December 1951 after departure of the 21.00 train to Shirebrook, with the goods facilities lasting until 4th March 1957. The station buildings were finally demolished in 1972 to make way for a new road. *Author's collection.*

This extremely rare photograph dating from about 1950 recently came to light, and shows a class J11 leaving Chesterfield Market Place with a long goods train. The viewpoint is from the Tube Works looking across to the Crooked Spire, and the works steam loco is in the foreground toying with wagons. The rear of the East Midland bus depot may be seen mid left. This is the only known shot of this part of the embankment with a train shown. *J. Cannam*

The final illustration from the L.D. & E.C. route comes from Calow just east of Chesterfield Market Place in 1956. This is a view not seen by many people, and is the western portal of Duckmanton Tunnel. The colour light is most unusual, and may have been the only one, certainly west of Shirebrook, unless of course, anyone knows otherwise. *D. Ibbotson*

THE NEW STEAM AGE — PRESERVED STEAM AT WORK ON BRITISH RAIL TRACKS IN THE NORTH MIDLANDS.

May 1987 saw the return of steam to the Matlock line, when 7F No 53809 from Butterley was used on a train from Nottingham. Further runs followed throughout the summer, with the 7F sharing turns with 35028 and 75069. It is seen emerging from Lee Wood Tunnel near Cromford on the June working. Compare this view with that on page 49 taken some 50 years before.   *A. R. Kaye*

The August 1987 train to Matlock was hauled by Standard class 4 No 75069, seen after arrival. All locomotives made a second short return trip to Derby during the afternoon before returning to Nottingham at 18.10.

Jubilee 5593 'Kolhapur' has unfortunately been dogged by failures in recent months, and a Derby to Carnforth trip in the early summer of 1988 was no exception. The loco expired at Keighley some two hours after this rousing start from a signal check on the approach to Chesterfield.

Both A. R. Kaye.

The first of the 1987 excursions from Derby to Buxton took place on a warm Easter Saturday. No 5593 successfully made the trip after a delayed start, and is seen approaching Buxton in Ashwood Dale — the first steam seen here since March 1968.

The second run was made in October with the triumphant return of 8F No 48151. The locomotive performed magnificently, and is seen (top right) on the return journey at Chesterfield in fading light. Unfortunately B.R. decreed that the Buxton line was 'not up to passenger carrying standards' in 1988 so no further runs have been made. It did not, however, prevent full scale diversions of express trains via Ashwood Dale in February 1988, making nonsense of the above statement.

Shirebrook and Worksop depots held an open day in May 1987 and the first steam train since the end of the 1960's was seen on the Pye Bridge-Shireoaks route. (A special with 4472 used the line in 1969). No 53809 returning to Butterley, crossed Mansfield viaduct in the evening (bottom right) above the Market Place. This was the first southbound steam working for more than 20 years. No 4498 'Sir Nigel Gresley' followed some time later, but after dusk. *All: A. R. Kaye*

The 'South Yorkshireman' specials from London to Sheffield have proved a major attraction in 1988. A northbound run in June featured class 5 No 5305 which was being worked to Scotland. It is seen swinging away from Lockoford Lane at Chesterfield on the 'Old Road' route via Beighton. The train returned to London behind the ever popular 'West Country' Pacific No 34092 'City of Wells', seen in surroundings not unfamiliar with its old stamping ground in Devon. It is actually sweeping past the site of Broomhouse Tunnel near Sheepbridge.

Both A. R. Kaye